Comfortable Wo

The Bible Reading Fellowship
15 The Chambers, Vineyard
Abingdon OX14 3FE
brf.org.uk

The Bible Reading Fellowship (BRF) is a Registered Charity (233280)

ISBN 978 1 80039 105 5
First published 2021
10 9 8 7 6 5 4 3 2 1 0
All rights reserved

Acknowledgements
Unless otherwise stated, scripture quotations are taken from The New Revised Standard Version of the Bible, Anglicised edition, copyright © 1989, 1995 by the Division of Christian Education of the National Council of the Churches of Christ in the United States of America. Used by permission. All rights reserved.

Scripture quotations marked KJV are taken from the Authorised Version of the Bible (The King James Bible), the rights in which are vested in the Crown, are reproduced by permission of the Crown's Patentee, Cambridge University Press.

'Read All About It (Part III)'. Words and Music by Iain James, Thomas Barnes, Peter Kelleher, Benjamin Kohn, Emeli Sande and Stephen Manderson. © Copyright 2012 Sony/ATV Music Publishing (UK) Limited/Stellar Songs Limited, Sony/ATV Music Publishing (UK) Limited/ EMI Music Publishing Limited and Bucks Music Group LTD. All Rights Reserved. International Copyright Secured. Used by Permission of Hal Leonard Europe Limited and Bucks Music Group LTD.

'Take Me to the Alley'. Author and Composer: Gregory Porter © Golden Slipper Publishing. With the kind authorisation of Universal Music Publishing.

Every effort has been made to trace and contact copyright owners for material used in this resource. We apologise for any inadvertent omissions or errors, and would ask those concerned to contact us so that full acknowledgement can be made in the future.

A catalogue record for this book is available from the British Library

Printed and bound by TJ Books

Steven Croft

Comfortable Words

a call to restoration

Reflections on Isaiah 40—55

To the clergy, lay ministers, church wardens and volunteers
of the Diocese of Oxford,
for your outstanding and inspiring service over the past year.

Contents

Introduction

At the beginning of the Covid-19 pandemic, as the country went into lockdown, I spent some time thinking about how best to sustain the church across the diocese in the coming months. No one knew, of course, how long the pandemic would last or what the effects would be in those early weeks.

By the grace of God, I made two early decisions with colleagues which proved helpful. The first was to develop an online service for the Diocese of Oxford every Sunday to support local churches who were already moving online. The second was to begin, tentatively, a regular podcast reflection on a passage of scripture. The podcast was aimed primarily at supporting and sustaining clergy and lay leaders of all kinds as we made this journey together.

The lockdown began on 23 March. Between May and July, I paid virtual visits to all 29 deaneries and met online with between 500 and 600 clergy and lay leaders. Each conversation was deeply moving. There was a tremendous outpouring of energy, creativity and love and the deep renewal of pastoral ministry which, taken together, was one of the most remarkable moves of God I have ever seen. But there were also signs that people were indeed carrying heavy burdens in their own lives, in their families, in their churches and in the wider community. That experience of listening also fed into the writing and delivery of the weekly podcast.

At the centre of the calling of a priest (and a bishop) is the service of the word and the prayers (to use the language of Acts 6). For much of the past year, apart from a short period in September and October, I was unable to keep to my normal pattern of preaching and leading worship in churches across the diocese. I tried to use that time to reflect at depth on a particular passage of scripture and to share it through the podcast.

The first series of reflections was on the Psalms, exploring themes of lament and suffering in particular.

The second was on Philippians, taking us deeper into what it means to be a church patterned on the character of Christ. Those reflections formed the core of a new study guide for churches, published in September.

The third series of podcasts took the songs of the unknown prophet of Isaiah 40—55, the voice crying in the wilderness, as its theme. This prophet sings at the end of the exile in Babylon, to call the people back to God, to give them strength again and to prepare the exiles for the work of rebuilding that would come. The songs are a deep well from which we can drink as a church in this most demanding of seasons.

I originally wrote and delivered one each week between September and the end of November 2020. At the beginning, churches were able to meet together physically, but most also continued to offer online as well as in-person worship. By the end of the series, we had walked through the second lockdown and looked forward to emerging gradually into a very different Advent and Christmas season.

The prophet's themes are powerful and relevant to the journey through Covid-19 and beyond. There are songs of great comfort and consolation; songs about leadership, especially the leadership of God's people; songs about facing difficulty and danger; and songs of purpose and about our calling and the rhythm of our discipleship.

The book of Isaiah isn't always easy to read, but it repays deep and careful study, as I have found over many years. As you work your way through these reflections, have the text open and listen carefully to the prophet's songs.

The songs will be relevant to the life of the church for many months to come, as we emerge from the lockdown period in both church and society and have the opportunity to reset and rebuild for the future. I'm grateful therefore to BRF for agreeing to publish these Comfortable Words in time to be a resource to a wider audience.

I want to thank very warmly indeed Steven Buckley, who produced the podcasts each week amid everything else he had to do. I also want to thank my senior colleagues in the diocese and my immediate team of Marian Green, Paul Cowan, Simon Cross and Sharon Appleton, who helped to create the time and space for this kind of writing and reflection (and so much else). Thanks as well to everyone who took the trouble to encourage me on this journey.

Most of all, I want to thank the clergy, lay ministers, church wardens, church officers and volunteers of the Diocese of Oxford, who, quite simply, have been outstanding and inspiring in churches, chaplaincies, schools and the wider community over this past year.

May God continue to be with us and to guide us all in the vital work of rebuilding to which we are now called.

Steven Croft, Oxford
Advent 2020

1

Comfort, O comfort my people

– Isaiah 40:1–11 –

At the closing ceremony of the London 2012 Olympic Games, Emeli Sandé sang 'Read All About It, Pt III', a song about finding strength and courage. We need to hear it even more now than we did then, as a church and as a nation:

> Let's get the TV and the radio to play our tune again
> It's 'bout time we got some airplay of our version of events
> There's no need to be afraid, I will sing with you my friend
> Come on, come on

I'll come back to the words later.

Sometimes a song, a play or a film will catch a moment and speak to a whole nation, sometimes to the whole world for a few weeks or a few years. Sometimes a song will speak to more than one generation. Just a small number of songs or poems in the entire history of human culture have spoken to the whole world across countless generations.

Five hundred years or so before the birth of Christ, there was such a song – or rather a collection of songs, an album if you like. We don't know the original tunes now. We only have the words. These beautiful songs were forged in a crucible of great suffering but also in a moment of great hope, at the end of the exile of the people of Israel in Babylon. In 587BC, Jerusalem was destroyed. Many of the people were taken captive and transported thousands of miles from their home on foot to modern-day Iraq. They lived and settled there. Their poets and prophets helped them understand how to sing the Lord's song in a strange land. Seventy years and several generations of hurt and suffering passed by.

Towards the end of the exile, a new prophet appeared, in the early dawn by the banks of the Tigris and Euphrates, singing to the exiles. This prophet doesn't have a name. He or she calls themselves a voice. His – or perhaps her – songs are collected together in 16 chapters of the book of Isaiah: chapters 40—55. They are songs that have changed the world.

In this series of reflections, I invite you to explore this rich collection of songs and what God might be saying to us through scripture in this unique and demanding season. We are seeking to find strength and hope amid so much uncertainty. This chapter focuses on the songs in Isaiah 40:1–11. The prophet begins with these powerful and beautiful words which sum up God's call to the exiles and to the church in every generation:

> Comfort, O comfort my people,
>   says your God.
> Speak tenderly to Jerusalem
>   and cry to her
> that she has served her term,
>   that her penalty is paid,
> that she has received from the Lord's hand
>   double for all her sins.

A voice cries out:
'In the wilderness prepare the way of the Lord,
    make straight in the desert a highway for our God.
Every valley shall be lifted up,
    and every mountain and hill be made low;
the uneven ground shall become level,
    and the rough places a plain.
Then the glory of the Lord shall be revealed,
    and all people shall see it together,
    for the mouth of the Lord has spoken.'
ISAIAH 40:1–5

That first line alone stands over the whole collection of songs and reso-nates down the centuries: 'Comfort, O comfort my people... Speak ten-derly.' Literally this means speak to the heart of Jerusalem or, even better, speak healings to the heart of Jerusalem, according to the earliest Greek translation.

The words are therefore a summons to gentleness, strength and hope. They mark a radical change of tone from the earlier prophets of the exile, Jeremiah and Ezekiel. These two earlier prophets analyse the problem and offer solutions and, in Ezekiel's case, great visions of hope. But here a line is drawn under all the suffering. The accent is on forgiveness, warmth and understanding. Comfort, comfort my people.

The word 'comfort' is used in the Hebrew Bible for words offered to the grieving and the broken. The word is used often of God, often describing God's change of mind and heart out of compassion for the needy.

The person and teaching of Jesus echo so much from these songs. Handel's *Messiah* begins its telling of the story of Jesus exactly here, with these words: 'Comfort my people.' Mark, the earliest gospel, raises the curtain on the ministry of Jesus by echoing Isaiah 40: 'The voice of one crying out in the wilderness: "Prepare the way of the Lord, make his paths straight"' (Mark 1:3). The rock musical *Godspell* begins in most productions with John the Baptist singing out this very song: 'Prepare ye the way of the Lord.'

In John's gospel, when Jesus looks for a name, a title, for the Holy Spirit, he settles on the Comforter (KJV; in the Greek *parakletos*), the one who draws alongside (John 14:16, 26; 15:26; 16:7). John is using exactly the same word as in the Greek version of Isaiah. The word can sometimes mean intercessor, the one who prays on our behalf, the Holy Spirit praying within us. It also means helper, the one who strengthens us, who helps us stand. There is a direct line from 'Comfort my people' to the Holy Spirit as comforter.

At the beginning of 2 Corinthians, Paul echoes Isaiah 40 again and reminds us how much this ministry of comfort and consolation is at the heart of the nature of God and therefore at the heart of our calling as Christians and of all Christian ministry:

> Blessed be the God and Father of our Lord Jesus Christ, the Father of mercies and the God of all consolation, who consoles us in all our affliction, so that we may be able to console those who are in any affliction with the consolation with which we ourselves are consoled by God.
> 2 CORINTHIANS 1:3–4

Again, the word is the same. Every mention of that word 'consolation' echoes and re-echoes the song of Isaiah 40: 'comfort my people'. Speak the good news of forgiveness. Prepare the way of the Lord.

What does it mean to listen to these comfortable words today – as the people of the God of all comfort; as the ones who follow Jesus, who speaks words of consolation; as the community which has been blessed with the

Holy Spirit, the Comforter, who dwells in our hearts through faith? We are, like the rest of the world around us, still grieving and confused at what has been happening during the Covid-19 pandemic. We are afraid of illness, death, hardship and a different future from the one we previously envisaged. We are overwhelmed sometimes by the changes which keep on happening and we long, of course, for life to be back to some kind of normal. We are confused about how best to navigate this time as individuals, as families, as a church and as ministers.

These songs are such a good place to begin to recentre our calling and to find strength and hope again. Yes, it has been and is hard and devastating to get up after the storm has passed, to begin to gather again as communities and to piece together our lives, not knowing when and if the same turbulence will come again.

But this song will help us to stand and also know how to be and what to say in angry and confusing times. Make no mistake, this is our calling as the church: to speak tenderly, to speak words of healing to the heart, to draw alongside others, physically and virtually, as God draws alongside us. That comfort will sometimes be practical, as we continue to offer shelter, food parcels or advice and support. It may simply be a smile, an encouraging word, a phone call or a note. 'Comfort my people,' says your God.

It is our calling to speak words of forgiveness. It's a message the world needs to hear as people reassess their lives and their priorities; as families are divided; as we become aware of our own failings in testing times; as churches fall apart, sometimes over the most trivial of matters. We need all of us to be messengers of forgiveness, to spread the word that God is a God of love and patience and is always ready to mend and forgive.

Isaiah 40 speaks to a people in a particular time and place: cry to her that her penalty is paid, that she has received from the Lord double for all her sins. The church has the joy and responsibility of proclaiming God's forgiveness in every time and place, because of the gift of Jesus Christ and the power of Christ's own death on the cross. He gave his life to offer the ultimate consolation; the offer of forgiveness, new life and salvation through faith is his gift to us. The very heart of our calling as disciples is to proclaim that forgiveness as grace and gift and to proclaim God's love in all circumstances and for every life.

It is our calling to prepare the way of the Lord, to be ambassadors for God in every place and situation in the physical world and the virtual world, so that amid all the anger, fear and confusion, people will begin to hear, perhaps distantly at first, the song of God's love and hope calling them home. It is our calling as the church to clear the way, to make the paths straight again, to lift up the valleys and make the mountains low again, and to make the uneven ground level, so that people can return to God and recover faith and the full measure of what it means to be human.

This is our calling, unworthy as we are: to point beyond ourselves, the material world and the busyness of life to eternal realities and the power, majesty and mercy of God.

This is God's song to us now, tired and worn out as we are: to comfort God's people, to prepare the way of the Lord, to proclaim forgiveness, to shout from the mountaintops the eternal majesty of God our maker.

When everyone around us is overwhelmed by the detail, we are to be the ones who listen to the word of God, the message of salvation, and find there a still centre and strength to change the world:

> The grass withers, the flower fades;
>> but the word of our God will stand forever.
> ISAIAH 40:8

Thousands of miles and three generations from Jerusalem, this wonder-ful prophet listens deeply to God and finds hope which still speaks to the world 2,500 years into the future. Listen:

> Get you up to a high mountain,
>> O Zion, herald of good tidings;
> lift up your voice with strength,
>> O Jerusalem, herald of good tidings,
>> lift it up, do not fear;
> say to the cities of Judah,
>> 'Here is your God!'...
> He will feed his flock like a shepherd;
>> he will gather the lambs in his arms,
> and carry them in his bosom,
>> and gently lead the mother sheep.
> ISAIAH 40:9, 11

Hear the notes of power and beauty there, but also the notes of tenderness, gentleness and healing.

How are we to hear this song today, as God calls to us across the ages, from the banks of the Euphrates in Babylon to the banks of the Thames or the Hudson or the Humber today?

The message I hear from the scriptures is this: God calls us even in the midst of crisis to find our voice again as disciples and as a church. We are to find our voice not for our own sake, but for the sake of our nation, the world and the communities we serve. We are to listen again to the gospel we live and bear, to find our strength and courage there again, to relearn our song in this strange land. In Emeli Sandé's words:

Let's get the TV and the radio to play our tune again
It's about time we got some airplay of our version of events
There's no need to be afraid, I will sing with you my friend
Come on, come on

And then we have to sing, through actions, prayers, words and worship, in every place and in every way we can, this song which Isaiah 40 teaches us again. The song of comfort, healing and forgiveness. The song of gentleness and consolation. The song which prepares the way of the Lord.

We must sing it in workplaces, in schools, in virtual gatherings, in village churches and cathedrals, in face masks, in the open air. We must recall the nation to the heart and rhythm of God, to what matters, to meaning and truth.

Comfort, O comfort my people,
   says your God
Speak tenderly to Jerusalem,
   and cry to her
that she has served her term,
   that her penalty is paid,
that she has received from the Lord's hand
   double for all her sins.

A voice cries out:
'In the wilderness prepare the way of the Lord;
   make straight in the desert a highway for our God.'

2

Those who wait for the Lord will renew their strength

– Isaiah 40:18–31 –

This is the world we live in. We live in a vulnerable world. One of the ways we deal with it is that we numb vulnerability. I think there's evidence – it's not the reason this evidence exists but it's a huge cause – we are the most in-debt, obese, addicted and medicated adult cohort in US history.

Those words are by Brené Brown, the American researcher and author, speaking in 2010 in what has become one of the most-viewed TED talks of all time, 'The power of vulnerability' (**ted.com/talks/brene_brown_the_power_of_vulnerability**). If you've not seen it, take 20 minutes to watch it.

Brown is attempting to describe the way the world around us has learned to respond to suffering, pain and difficulty. The temptation is to numb all of this negative emotion, to overlay it, to disguise it through shopping, social media, food, alcohol or other addictive behaviours. We numb.

In normal times that can set in motion slow but destructive cycles of behaviour in our lives. We keep afloat, but only just. In times of crisis and difficulty, however, it is not enough to numb. The pain around us over-whelms our defences. Something much deeper is needed.

By the rivers of Babylon, 2,500 years ago, there was a prophet who called himself – or herself – a voice crying in the wilderness, a prophet without a name. The call of this prophet is to bring comfort to the people of Israel, in exile far from home. The songs of the prophet have been passed down to us in 16 beautiful chapters of the book of Isaiah, chapters 40—55.

The prophet is called to bring comfort. That call to comfort gives us the opening line of the first song. But this was comfort with a purpose. The prophet's aim – and the Lord's aim – is not simply to soothe the exiles and dry their tears, though the songs are songs of great tenderness and hope. The people of God are downcast and defeated by three generations of exile.

The prophet's vision, however, is much bigger. It is to regather the people of God, to help them, first of all, to stand again, to give them strength and purpose and to remind them of who they are. And then it is to put courage, fight, faith and joy back into their hearts.

God is leading the exiles home again to Jerusalem, to rebuild the nation and the temple. That will soon become possible for the first time in 70 years. But will they choose to go? How many will make the journey? To make that great return they will need all their strength again. The exiles must therefore be recalled to God and to their faith, must find their strength and hope if they are to stand, return and rebuild.

These exiles have spent two generations in Babylon. They have experienced hardship, but also all kinds of pleasures and temptations. All around them are the temples of the gods of Babylon, the idols, projections of human ideas and power. The worship of the idols is designed exactly to numb the exiles, to help them forget the living God, to seduce them into merging with the population around them. If they had done so, the entire history of the world would have been so very different.

So our prophet sings to call them back, to remind them of a better way. The songs are not telling the exiles anything new. This is recall and remembering, not new information.

We are recalled first to the beauty and majesty of God in creation:

> Who has measured the waters in the hollow of his hand
>   and marked off the heavens with a span,
> enclosed the dust of the earth in a measure,
>   and weighed the mountains in scales
>   and the hills in a balance.
> ISAIAH 40:12

The God of Israel is not one god among many, as it must have seemed to the exiles amid the temples of Babylon. The God of Israel is God Almighty, the maker of the heavens and the earth, the only God. The whole beauty, order and majesty of creation tells us that God has wisdom, skill and power beyond our comprehension.

The God of Israel is not a god manufactured or invented by humans, crafted from wood by a carpenter and decorated by a goldsmith.

> To whom then will you liken God,
>   or what likeness compare with him?

An idol? – A workman casts it
    and a goldsmith overlays it with gold,
    and casts for it silver chains.
ISAIAH 40:18–19

When we pursue idols, we are pursuing gods made with human hands, limited by our own imagination, who cannot lead us home.

True purpose, meaning and strength do not lie in this direction, sings the voice. For there is an older, deeper story. You have heard it in your youth. Your deepest being longs for this song to be true. Listen to the call:

Have you not known? Have you not heard?
    Has it not been told you from the beginning?
    Have you not understood from the foundations of the earth?
It is he who sits above the circle of the earth,
    and its inhabitants are like grasshoppers;
who stretches out the heavens like a curtain,
    and spreads them like a tent to live in.
ISAIAH 40:21–22

God the creator is real and strong and calling out to God's people to stand and rebuild.

How will God's people respond? Will we hide away, turn inwards, full of our fear, misery and resentment?

Why do you say, O Jacob,
    and speak O Israel,
'My way is hidden from the Lord,
    and my right is disregarded by my God'?
ISAIAH 40:27

Again the prophet recalls us:

> Have you not known? Have you not heard?
> The Lord is the everlasting God...

This time the prophet uses the personal name of God, the name revealed to Moses, the name his people will not pronounce. The God of Israel is the one true Almighty God, the maker of heaven and earth.

> The Lord is the everlasting God
>   the Creator of the ends of the earth.
> He does not faint or grow weary;
>   his understanding is unsearchable.
> ISAIAH 40:28

The exiles may feel small and forgotten. They may be worn down by life's hardships and distracted by the temptations around them. They may be burdened by their own weakness and the sin of their nation. They may feel they have fallen, never to rise again.

But the prophet's song fills their hearts and minds with a vision of God who is deeper and greater, a God beyond time and the universe, a prime mover and a sustainer, a God of majesty and power, way beyond the game of thrones and clash of empires in which their lives are trapped. This God is calling them.

The prophet moves to the song's ending:

> He gives power to the faint,
>   and strengthens the powerless.
> Even youths will faint and be weary,
>   and the young will fall exhausted;

but those who wait for the Lord shall renew their strength,
    they shall mount up with wings like eagles,
they shall run and not be weary,
    they shall walk and not faint.
ISAIAH 40:29–31

Which way will we turn, I wonder, in this time and season as we continue to walk through all of the confusion and pain around us? We need to recognise our own history. For every generation for the past 70 years, the tide of faith has gone out a little further. Each generation has inherited fewer and fewer resources from our Christian heritage for coping with grief, pain and difficulty. It has come as a deep shock to some younger generations in the pandemic that things can go so badly wrong so quickly. As Christians we can be caught up in the spirit of the age. We can forget the strength, resilience and life that come from our faith and ultimately from God. We need to be recalled.

'Have you not known. Have you not heard,' the prophet says to us.

Much of the society around us does not know what to do with pain and difficulty, even in normal times. We try to deaden our emotions, to numb, to use Brené Brown's words. Here is the quotation again, with slightly more included this time:

> This is the world we live in. We live in a vulnerable world. One of the ways we deal with it is that we numb vulnerability. I think there's evidence – it's not the reason this evidence exists but it's a huge cause – we are the most in debt, obese, addicted and medicated adult cohort in US history.
>   The problem is – and I learned this from the research – you cannot selectively numb emotion. You cannot say, 'Here's the bad stuff: here's vulnerability, here's grief, here's shame, here's disappointment.

I don't want to feel these. I'm going to have a couple of beers and a banana nut muffin. I don't want to feel these'... You can't select those. So when we numb those we numb joy, we numb gratitude, we numb happiness. Then we are miserable, and we are looking for purpose and meaning and we feel vulnerable. So then we have a couple of beers and a banana nut muffin – and it becomes this dangerous cycle.

The prophet of Isaiah 40 encourages us not to numb but to acknowledge pain, difficulty and suffering and then, still, to open our hearts to God's love, healing and strength. In God's light and love we are given the strength to face the pain and questions because of this greater and deeper reality and hope and love. This is what it means to wait on the Lord. This waiting is more than taking time to say our prayers, though time is certainly involved. It is time to listen to the pain and difficulty within us and the world around us and to open that pain to God's grace and healing.

In Isaiah 40 we are to open our hearts to the Lord first through the beauty and majesty of the creation. The size, beauty and majesty of the universe point us, if we will look, to the God of order, beauty and purpose. This world did not come about by chance or accident. Our longing for something beyond ourselves, for love and meaning, would be the strangest product of random evolution, but it makes absolute sense if, as scripture tells us, we were made to acknowledge and to know our maker.

As Christians we are called to ponder the mystery of God in the book of creation, to be recalled to our insignificance but also to the wonder that God cares for and loves us as individuals.

But we are also called to ponder the mystery of God as revealed in scripture and, most of all, in Jesus, God's Son. Our prophet will thread references to the word of God through almost every song. The prophet goes on to sing of the servant of the Lord who will come and show us more of God's nature and bring healing through his own suffering, as we will see.

Those who wait for the Lord shall renew their strength. They shall run and not be weary. They shall walk and not faint.

Many of us find it hard to be still, to have an empty day or a couple of hours when we are not sure what to do. We are restless. One of the reasons for our restlessness is that when we stop, when we allow space, all of the pain and questions rise to the surface.

Our society needs more space and time for this, not less. Carrying so much pain and turmoil within is exhausting. We need the courage to stop, to listen, to be ourselves, to sit for a while and to find those moments of renewal when we hear God speak.

That can happen in our prayers, in our worship, in the silence of our empty churches, in the sunshine. I went for a bike ride on a Saturday morning down the canal path towards Oxford. By the side of the path, I passed a woman sitting cross-legged on the ground, her face turned towards the sun. I've no idea, of course, what was happening inside her. But it seemed to me that here was someone who was waiting on the Lord to renew her strength, who was recognising all that was happening, who was seeking that grace and strength from God to rise up and rebuild.

> Even youths will faint and be weary,
>   and the young will fall exhausted;
> but those who wait for the Lord shall renew their strength,
>   they shall mount up with wings like eagles,
> they shall run and not be weary,
>   they shall walk and not faint.

3

Do not be afraid

– Isaiah 41:8–13 –

What's your favourite comedy? At the moment, mine is probably *W1A*. ('So that's all good, then.') But I grew up with *Dad's Army*. Written by Jimmy Perry and David Croft (sadly no relation), 80 episodes were broadcast between 1968 and 1977. I was between 11 and 20. I think I've seen most of them, but probably not all.

Looking back, I guess *Dad's Army* struck a chord for my parents' generation, who had lived through World War II. It was a way of coming to terms with the immense tragedy and suffering of the war years and finding healing through laughter. As is the way with sitcoms, the different characters offer different ways of responding to the same situation. We see ourselves reflected back in different shades. How would we have responded to fear and danger and the questions asked by war? How are we responding now?

It's interesting but not surprising that so many of the responses in *Dad's Army* are marked by fear. 'Don't panic,' shouts Corporal Jones. His fear is infectious and, of course, leads to people running around like headless chickens. 'We're doomed, Captain Mainwaring,' says Private Frazer, spreading despair and sapping the limited strength of the platoon. 'May

I be excused?' says Private Godfrey, creeping away from the back of the line. 'Are you sure that's really wise, sir?' asks the gentle Sergeant Wilson, the most valuable member of the leadership team (but perhaps that's not saying very much).

Fear is our unwelcome and sometimes unacknowledged companion in most situations of crisis and in many different parts of our lives. In its acute forms, fear prevents people getting out of bed in the morning. Anxiety strips joy away from families. Fear prevents relationships forming. We worry about what's going to happen, about what people think. Social media being available 24/7 has undoubtedly raised anxiety levels among the young. The 2020 Netflix film *The Social Dilemma* documents the addictive and destructive effects of new technology. Many of us fall victim to 'the fear of missing out' (FOMO) – the belief that everyone else is having a good time.

Fear has been a feature of our journey through Covid-19: fear of the disease itself and its consequences; fear of death and dying; fear of the effects on our families. Some of that fear is rational. Covid is a dreadful disease, which has killed so many, as is evident from the daily figures that have been reported since March 2020. Some fear, however, is irrational. Fear multiplies itself within us and in others and often goes beyond what is justified, stripping away our capacity to act. Fear has characterised some of the meetings I've been part of through the pandemic and some of the decision-making processes, even though that fear has not always been named.

We are exploring in this book the songs of the unknown prophet who sang to the exiles in Babylon 2,500 years ago. The prophet sings to bring God's comfort and strength to the people. The songs are preserved for us in Isaiah 40—55.

It will soon be time for the exiles to return. They will need to look to the future and to hope in order to make the journey back to Jerusalem and to rebuild. In the previous reflection, we saw the ways in which the prophet seeks to bring strength to the people by pointing them to the song of creation, to the strength and power of the living God: those who wait on the Lord shall renew their strength.

In Isaiah 41, the prophet's song moves on from the themes of comfort, hope and renewal to address this paralysing fear in the hearts and lives of the exiles. The people of God have lived for decades as refugees. Perhaps in some ways they have become comfortable. But they have no security. At any time, those around them might turn on them. How are they to find confidence to rebuild, still less to make the journey back to Jerusalem?

Listen to the tender way in which God speaks to them through the prophet's song:

> But you, Israel, my servant,
>   Jacob, whom I have chosen,
>   the offspring of Abraham, my friend.
> ISAIAH 41:8

Let's just pause there for a moment and hear what's being said. Wouldn't that be wonderful if Almighty God could address us in that way – if God were to reach out to us and call us his servants, his chosen ones and his friends?

That is exactly what God is doing in Christ. Jesus says, 'I do not call you servants any longer... but I have called you friends' (John 15:15). So the words of Isaiah 41:8 are ones we can hear in our situation, addressed to us as we walk through this present darkness. These words of gentleness and love: my servant, my chosen, my friend. Take a moment to hear God speaking those words to you.

The prophet continues:

> You whom I took from the ends of the earth,
>> and called from its farthest corners…

Nowhere is beyond God's reach, God's gaze and God's love.

> … saying to you, 'You are my servant,
>> I have chosen you and not cast you off.'
> ISAIAH 41:9

There's a sense of God calling out to Israel, who looks over her shoulder and says, 'Who, me? You can't mean us, surely. We've failed you, Lord. We come from nowhere. Our home is at the ends of the earth. Babylon is the centre of the world now. We are captives in a foreign country. Our families let you down. We are just a scattered group of exiles now. You can't mean us. You probably hardly even remember us and our ancestors.'

> … saying to you, 'You are my servant,
>> I have chosen you and not cast you off.'

God takes some time to gain Israel's attention, and when God has their attention, this is what he says, the entire message of Isaiah 41:

> Do not fear, for I am with you,
>> do not be afraid, for I am your God;
> I will strengthen you, I will help you,
>> I will uphold you with my victorious right hand.
> ISAIAH 41:10

A few verses further on, he says:

> For I, the Lord your God,
>   hold your right hand;
> it is I who say to you: 'Do not fear,
>   I will help you.'
> ISAIAH 41:13

And for a third time:

> Do not fear, you worm Jacob,
>   you insect Israel!
> I will help you, says the Lord;
>   your Redeemer is the Holy One of Israel.
> ISAIAH 41:14

Listen to this, my servant, my chosen, my friend: do not be afraid, for I am your God.

How should we hear the prophet's song? Perhaps the first step is to hear and acknowledge our own fears. One of the strange things about fear is that not only does it imprison us, but, like the exiles, we also perhaps grow used to our captivity. Living as the prisoner of fear becomes normal, so much so that we forget our chains.

One of the most powerful moments in *The Lord of the Rings* trilogy is when Gandalf sets free Théoden, king of Rohan. Théoden is a man who has been taken prisoner by fear, whispered in his ear by his devious servant Wormtongue. Over many years, Wormtongue has magnified the dangers and the forces of evil and has whispered despair into the heart of the king, sapping his strength, cutting him off from the light and making him a prisoner of anxiety and fear. Théoden has grown so used to these chains of despair that he no longer realises they are there until Gandalf releases him and restores him to life.

It was no doubt the same with the exiles, and it can be the same with us. Our fears multiply, perhaps especially so in uncertain and dangerous times. We do not realise that we are even afraid or the ways our fears are drawing off our energy and strength.

So perhaps I can ask you to look back over the past year and reflect for a moment. What part has fear played in your own life and your life's journey? What part is anxiety playing now in the key decisions of your life? Does it have too loud a voice? Does all of that fear and caution have the support of reason? Are there inner fears which you are keeping buried deep inside and cannot name or talk through with those closest to you? Are those chains of fear shaping the decisions you make in your work or your Christian service?

If that is the case, listen to the word of the Lord to you:

> Do not fear, for I am with you,
>   do not be afraid, for I am your God;
> I will strengthen you, I will help you,
>   I will uphold you with my victorious right hand.

We recognise, we remember and we name our fears and bring them into the light of God's love. At the same time, through the songs of the prophet, we remember whose we are. We remember who God is: God's majesty, God's love, God's salvation in Christ, God's love for us despite our failings and weaknesses, God's promise of support.

There are many passages to explore on that theme, including the journey of the exiles, but I am drawn again and again in reading this prophet to the last discourses of Jesus in John's gospel. We saw in chapter 1 the way in which Jesus names the Holy Spirit as the Comforter, echoing the Greek of Isaiah 40, where the prophet sings, 'Comfort my people.' In those same final discourses, Jesus speaks of the gift of the Holy Spirit to dwell within the heart of the believer. God sets his Spirit within us:

> The [Comforter], the Holy Spirit, whom the Father will send in my name, will teach you everything, and remind you of all that I have said to you. Peace I leave with you; my peace I give to you… Do not let your hearts be troubled, and do not let them be afraid.
> JOHN 14:26–27

On the evening of the first Easter Day, this is how Jesus describes the gift of the Holy Spirit to the first disciples (remember that they are afraid; the doors are locked, for fear of the Jews):

> Jesus said to them again, 'Peace be with you. As the Father has sent me, so I send you.' When he had said this, he breathed on them and said to them, 'Receive the Holy Spirit.'
> JOHN 20:21–22

Anyone who reads anything about the history of the church will know that the church from time to time has needed to remember this great treasure of the gift of the Holy Spirit, God, dwelling in our heart, driving away fear, releasing us from anxiety and giving us the hearts of lions again, as well as courage to live out and bear witness to our faith and to follow where God leads.

You might think we have moved on some way now from Isaiah 41, but that is not the case. One of the most powerful images for the Holy Spirit in John's gospel is drawn directly from this prophet. In John 7, Jesus stands up on the last and greatest day of the festival and cries out:

'Let anyone who is thirsty come to me, and let the one who believes in me drink. As the scripture has said, "Out of the believer's heart shall flow rivers of living water."' Now he said this about the Spirit, which believers in him were to receive; for as yet there was no Spirit, because Jesus was not yet glorified.

JOHN 7:37–39

Jesus is echoing Isaiah 55:1 and also 58:11. But in our passage as well, after the threefold command not to be afraid, this is what our prophet sings:

When the poor and needy seek water
    and there is none,
    and their tongue is parched with thirst,
I the Lord will answer them,
    I the God of Israel will not forsake them.
I will open rivers on the bare heights,
    and fountains in the midst of the valleys;
I will make the wilderness a pool of water,
    and the dry land springs of water.

ISAIAH 41:17–18

God is in the business of turning deserts into springs of living water, especially the dry places of our hearts.

As a church, our hearts are dry and we will need again a new Pentecost for this season.

In the middle of the pandemic, between the first two lockdowns in England, I was privileged to share in two services on the same day. In one of the parishes in Oxford, it was an enormous privilege to baptise and confirm two older teenagers and one adult into Christian faith and to confirm them and pray for them to receive the Holy Spirit (all in a socially distanced way).

In another it was again an immense privilege to ordain four new deacons, delayed from the previous June, as part of a season of ordinations in which many gifted new ministers have been ordained to the ministry of God's church. I thank God for them. They did not have the easiest of beginnings.

But my prayer throughout has been for the whole church, that we might recognise our fears, that we might hear God's word to us of comfort and of strength and that we might seek again the renewing grace and power of God's Spirit.

I finish with this great prayer, attributed to the ninth-century German arch-bishop Rabanus Maurus, which invites the Spirit to come into all our lives. Say it with me today and in the coming week:

> Come, Holy Ghost, our souls inspire,
>   and lighten with celestial fire;
> thou the anointing Spirit art,
>   who dost thy sevenfold gifts impart.
>
> Thy blessed unction from above
>   is comfort, life and fire of love;
> enable with perpetual light
>   the dullness of our blinded sight.
>
> Anoint and cheer our soiled face
>   with the abundance of thy grace.
> Keep far from foes, give peace at home;
>   where thou art guide, no ill can come.

Teach us to know the Father, Son
   and thee, of both, to be but One,
that through the ages all along,
   this may be our endless song:

Praise to thy eternal merit,
   Father, Son and Holy Spirit.
Amen

Servant leadership

– Isaiah 42:1–9 –

'The Servant Song (Brother, sister, let me serve you)' by Richard Gillard is one of the most popular contemporary worship songs and is sung by churches of many different traditions. It's often chosen for services of ordination and licensing new ministers. The song captures something vital about the way of discipleship. As Christians we are called to a life of service together, to love and support one another in all the joys and sorrows of our lives.

Where does that idea come from? Of course, it comes from Jesus. Jesus famously washes the feet of his disciples in John 13. During his very last meal with his friends, Jesus takes a towel and a basin of water and kneels before each of them in turn to wash the dust from their feet. Jesus then calls the disciples and us to do this for one another.

Jesus describes himself as a servant and invites those who would be leaders not to lord it over others but to seek to be servants of all. The word 'minister' derives from a Latin word that means, simply, servant. The Son of Man did not come to be served but to serve and to give his life as a ransom for many (see Mark 10:45).

Jesus frames his entire ministry around this idea of service, which sets others free to serve. From the earliest times in the church, this powerful, revolutionary notion reshapes the very idea of God and the relationship between the Father and the Son. The apostle Paul writes that Jesus:

> though he was in the form of God,
>> did not regard equality with God
>> as something to be exploited,
> but emptied himself,
>> taking the form of a slave,
>> being born in human likeness.
> PHILIPPIANS 2:6–7

The very idea of greatness, of leadership, is turned upside down. God is no longer a distorted projection of human ideas of power, but is radically different. Almighty God comes to us, takes flesh and becomes a slave, giving his own life to set others free in lives of service.

But where do these ideas first take shape? Remember Peter's reaction to the foot-washing. Peter thinks he knows who Jesus is: the Messiah, the Son of God. But Peter is offended at the idea of the Messiah, God's anointed, washing the dust from his feet. The people of Israel were expecting and hoping for a messiah who would be like one of the kings of old, a new David, who would take power in the conventional sense. This messiah would overthrow the Roman rulers by force. This messiah would establish a new kingdom in Jerusalem and, as it were, enforce peace and justice through all the earth. Peter's mind is offended at the idea of such a king kneeling before him with a basin of water, and he says to Jesus, 'You will never wash my feet' (John 13:8).

But there are two great strands of thinking about leadership and power in dialogue in the Old Testament. One is certainly the strand about kings establishing themselves by force and with glory and lording it over everyone else. All too often such power corrupts those who wield it, however glorious their intentions. Think of the long lists of the kings of Israel and Judah whose hearts became proud and turned away from the ways of the Lord.

The second strand is centred on humility: the meekness of Moses, God's servant, who was more humble 'than anyone else on the face of the earth' (Numbers 12:3); the humility of the young David, whose heart was open to God; the humility of Solomon at the beginning of his reign, when he sought not wealth, power or long life but the wisdom to govern the people of God and to bear the weight of his ministry.

It is this strand which finds its fullest expression in the Old Testament in the songs of our unnamed prophet, who calls themself a voice, who speaks to us from the book of Isaiah.

In Isaiah 40, we hear the prophet's call to comfort God's people and to call them back to hope and renewal as they prepare to return from exile. In Isaiah 41, the prophet seeks to cast out fear and anxiety and find water in the wilderness. In Isaiah 42, the prophet turns from unfolding the greatness of God and God's call to the kind of human agency and leadership that is needed to establish God's reign and God's kingdom. What kind of a leader do God's people need to help them realise their call in every generation?

This prophet speaks, remember, from a crucible of suffering and exile, when everything has been destroyed. There is now no king, no temple, no city of Zion, no gathered people of God; there are only exiles with a longing to go home. The great experiment of God's chosen people has, it seems, failed. Those who were entrusted with God's law rebelled and turned away. There have been multiple failures of leadership across many generations: of kings and prophets and priests and wise teachers. What kind of leadership is needed now in the place where everything needs to be rebuilt?

Our prophet is inspired by God to draw together the threads of this second great strand of thinking on leadership in the Old Testament. He or she weaves them into four songs which crystallise this vision: we will explore them all carefully in these reflections. Later generations have called them the Servant Songs. These are the prophecies that shape Jesus' own understanding of his call, his mission and his identity; they shape his ministry and go on to shape the church. This first song, in Isaiah 42:1–4, is quoted in full in Matthew 12:18–21. It is the longest single quotation from scripture in the entire gospel. Here is the passage from Isaiah:

> Here is my servant, whom I uphold,
>   my chosen, in whom my soul delights;
> I have put my spirit upon him;
>   he will bring forth justice to the nations.
> He will not cry or lift up his voice,
>   or make it heard in the street;
> a bruised reed he will not break,
>   and a dimly burning wick he will not quench;
>   he will faithfully bring forth justice.
> He will not grow faint or be crushed
>   until he has established justice in the earth;
>   and the coastlands wait for his teaching.
> ISAIAH 42:1–4

Every generation has debated the identity of the servant in these songs. In Acts 8, the Ethiopian eunuch in his chariot is reading one of the later songs and is stirred to wonder. He asks Philip: 'About whom… does the prophet say this, about himself or about someone else?' (Acts 8:34).

In much of Isaiah 40—55, the whole nation of Israel is called God's servant. But in these songs the language is more personal. The prophet is seeking to describe the role of those called to lead the people of God, especially the one whom God will call, in the fullness of time, to serve, guide and redeem the whole world. Every line, almost every word of the song, is worth weighing and pondering. As Matthew's gospel applies the whole text to Jesus in his ministry, so should we.

It is Jesus who is God's servant. The Greek word for servant is *pais*, which is also the ordinary Greek word for child or son. So another way of translating the Greek text is: 'Here is my Son, whom I uphold, my chosen, in whom my soul delights.' The other place in the gospels where there is a strong echo of this line is the account of Jesus' baptism:

> And a voice from heaven said: 'This is my Son, the Beloved, with whom I am well pleased.'
> MATTHEW 3:17

Here is an absolutely vital truth to grasp in terms of the words in Isaiah, in Jesus' own ministry and in the service that we ourselves offer. What is being described here is not drudgery, blind obedience or service out of compulsion or obligation. This is service rooted in a relationship of love and delight, service that is freely offered, service grounded in a call of God, service that may be difficult but which is also a source of rich joy.

> Here is my servant, whom I uphold,
>   my chosen, in whom my soul delights.

The prophet goes on to speak of the way in which the servant is commissioned and sustained. Again we sometimes have the idea that God gives his servants difficult tasks and then leaves them to get on with them. This is not the case here. God says clearly:

> I have put my spirit upon him;
>   he will bring forth justice to the nations.

Again, the accounts of Jesus' baptism echo this verse as they describe the Spirit descending on Jesus in bodily form like a dove. 'The Spirit of the Lord is upon me,' says a later prophet in Isaiah 61, words again quoted in Luke 4 by Jesus in the synagogue in Nazareth. Jesus ministers, serves and leads out of a close, sustaining, nurturing relationship with the Father and the Spirit. The life of God the Trinity is poured out in him and through him.

The aim of this ministry is caught in this word 'justice' (or social righteousness), which is repeated three times in the song: 'he will bring forth justice to the nations'; 'he will faithfully bring forth justice'; 'until he has established justice in the earth'.

The servant's ministry is not to one nation or community; it is for the sake of all the nations of the earth. In the words of the song that follows, God's call to the servant is to be:

… a covenant to the people,
a light to the nations,
to open the eyes that are blind,
to bring out the prisoners from the dungeon,
from the prison those who sit in darkness.
ISAIAH 42:6–7

This is justice, and justice is the biggest of words. It embraces the whole of setting the world to rights: healing the dislocation between the creator and the creation; providing a way for sins to be forgiven and humanity to be reconciled with God; establishing fairness in human society, be that in law, in politics and community life or in the economy; the good stewardship of creation and handing on the earth unharmed to future generations. It is hard to imagine a bigger, longer-lasting calling. It's one in which we all share.

The servant is rooted in a relationship of love and sustained by God; the servant is shaped by this all-encompassing vision of justice. How will the servant then reshape God's world? This is the central paradox of servant leadership: the call to transformation, not by force or conventional human power, but through gentleness and silence. As the prophet sings:

> He will not cry or lift up his voice,
>   or make it heard in the street;
> a bruised reed he will not break,
>   and a dimly burning wick he will not quench.

The servant's leadership will not overpower us. It will be characterised by meekness and kindness, for this is the very nature of God. It is a leadership that never gives up hope for individuals or for the world. It is a leadership that enables, and it is a leadership of love.

How we need this kind of leadership in the world and in the church in this season. We need this leadership as the world rebuilds after Covid. We need this leadership to empower and release the gifts of the church. We need this leadership as we wrestle with creating a safer church and continuing to care for the victims and survivors of abuse. We need this leadership as we explore and debate human sexuality and gender. The world has never been in greater need of this deep, healing stream of leadership, which exercises power with enormous caution, to heal and not to hurt, to build and not to destroy, preserving and not overwhelming the agency of others.

There is one further line to this first song, one more component of this servant leadership, and it is deeply unpopular and challenging. The servant is rooted in relationship with God, energised by this world-transforming mission, gentle and enabling. The servant also perseveres with costly and demanding ministry and sacrifice as an essential part of that mission to serve others:

He will not grow faint or be crushed
   until he has established justice in the earth;
   and the coastlands wait for his teaching.

There are two lessons here. The first is the need for perseverance in all forms of leadership. When life is demanding and difficult as a teacher, doctor, vicar, civil servant, churchwarden or charity CEO, it can be tempting to walk away. We all need strength and stickability in our leadership. The servant endures, by the grace of God.

But the second lesson is the cost of that. The servant bears the costly weight of leadership. This does not overwhelm God's servant, but that does not mean that it is without cost or easy to bear. He will not grow faint or be crushed until he has established justice. In every servant ministry there is cost and difficulty as well as endurance. The servant songs will develop this theme in much greater depth and detail as we read on.

By the rivers of Babylon so long ago, the prophet crafts a vision of leadership unlike anything the world has ever seen: leadership which takes its authority not from wealth or physical strength, armies or thrones. This is leadership which takes its authority from service and vocation in humility and gentleness. This is leadership rooted and grounded in the servant's relationship with God, the creator of all, and given vitality by the Spirit of God. This is leadership with the deepest and widest of horizons: establishing justice in and for the earth. This is leadership which perseveres and whose methods are tenderness, silence and care for individuals.

This is the vision of leadership fulfilled in Jesus, the servant. This is the leadership we are invited to exercise in our families, our communities and our churches.

5

When you pass through the waters, I will be with you

– Isaiah 43:1–7 –

One of the oldest books on my shelf is John Bunyan's *The Pilgrim's Progress*, the famous allegory of the Christian life, published over 300 years ago. The hymn 'Who would true valour see' is taken directly from his text. Bunyan was the pastor of an early non-conformist church in Bedford, an early Puritan. He spent over twelve years in prison for his beliefs. His life and ministry remain an influence particularly in South Buckinghamshire but also globally because of the abiding popularity of his story of Christian. *The Pilgrim's Progress* is rightly famous for the Giant Despair, the Slough of Despond, Vanity Fair and the burden of sin which rolls off Christian's back at the foot of the cross.

I first read Bunyan as a young Christian and have returned to *The Pilgrim's Progress* many times. One summer when I was a vicar, we preached a memorable series of all-age sermons on the different stages of the journey, and I remember clearly doing battle in the aisle of the church with the Giant

Despair and only just escaping. The book is probably best known now as an illustrated story for children. More recently, an animated film and a feature film, *Heavenquest: A Pilgrim's Progress*, have been released, though I have yet to see either of them.

At the end of Christian's journey, after many twists, turns and trials, he arrives at last at a great river, symbolising death. There is no bridge over this river and no way around it:

> Now I further saw that betwixt them and the Gate was a River, but there was no bridge to go over; the River was very deep; at the sight therefore of this River the pilgrims were much stounded, but the men that went with them said, 'You must come through or you cannot come at the Gate.'

Christian and Hopeful search for another way, but this river cannot be bypassed. Eventually they step into the flowing water. Christian begins to sink. Hopeful supports his friend. They quote scripture to one another until Christian says, at the very last:

> And he tells me: 'When thou passest through the waters, I will be with thee, and through the rivers they shall not overflow thee.' Then they both took courage and the enemy was after that as still as a stone, until they were gone over.

Christian (and Bunyan) offers this quotation in the face of death. It is from Isaiah 43, from the prophet who sings to us so many comfortable words. This is the full quotation:

> But now thus says the Lord,
>   he who created you, O Jacob,
>   he who formed you, O Israel:

Do not fear, for I have redeemed you;
   I have called you by name, you are mine.
When you pass through the waters, I will be with you;
   and through the rivers, they shall not overwhelm you;
when you walk through fire you shall not be burned,
   and the flame shall not consume you.
ISAIAH 43:1–2

The passage goes on to speak of the way God will ransom Israel and how much love God has for them:

Because you are precious in my sight,
   and honoured, and I love you.
ISAIAH 43:4

God will gather his people together again, scattered throughout the earth in their exile.

These are undoubtedly words of great comfort in their original context and every time they are read aloud in church today. The words are powerful ones to hear amid the pandemic. They would have been as powerful for the generation at the end of the exile.

God is speaking words of great comfort to God's people. Their punishment is over, their strength is returning, they are called to leave their fear behind, to rise up and journey back across the desert to their homes. They are to be led by a new kind of leader, the servant who will not break the bruised reed.

Many dangers may beset them on the way, but they will not be overwhelmed by the rivers or consumed by the flames. This is to be a new exodus, we read elsewhere. The seas will part before the Israelites so they can cross on dry land.

The prophecy was indeed fulfilled. The exiles did return and rebuild. But these words went on providing comfort and consolation to the people of God. The author of the stories in the book of Daniel may have had them in mind: remember the story of Shadrach, Meshach and Abednego and the fiery furnace, dating from a time of bitter persecution against the Jews.

But the interpretation offered by John Bunyan is the most natural one for Christians. It is enormous comfort to know that God loves us and will not abandon us in this life; that God is with us in all our trials; that the rivers will not overwhelm us and the fires will not consume us, whatever may happen.

But in the light of the death and resurrection of Christ, the words find their deepest meaning, as in Bunyan's story, as we prepare to face the last and greatest trial of our lives, the river which is death and our own mortality. The waters in the Old Testament are, more often than not, the waters of chaos and death, the floods that overwhelm us. This is life's final and greatest challenge to each of us. The prophet's song, in the light of our faith in Christ, is a deep song of reassurance in the face of our own mortality.

> When thou passest through the waters, I will be with thee; and through the rivers, they shall not overflow thee.
> ISAIAH 43:2 (KJV)

It was a great privilege during the lockdown to ordain new priests in the diocese. This year the ordinations were smaller, with just a small number of people gathered because of the restrictions, and with more watching online. Normally ordinations are large and grand affairs. I found these ordinations very moving, I think because they were so small. This was about the grace of God, the candidates and the ministry to which they were ordained. There is a passage in the service called the charge, which sets out the scope of the ministry of the priest. I was struck, in this time of Covid, by this phrase about the new priests' ministry:

They are to bless the people in God's name. They are to resist evil, support the weak, defend the poor and intercede for all in need. They are to minister to the sick and prepare the dying for their death.

It was the last part of that phrase which has stayed with me: 'They are to prepare the dying for their death.' This is part of priestly ministry. This is an area where each of us will need help and preparation. Bearing in mind the powerful song of Isaiah 43, what might it mean for each of us to be well prepared for death?

I received a number of letters during the lockdown period from people advising me that the church – and bishops – should be doing more in this area or in that. The ones I've had most sympathy with have been asking for a greater focus on exactly this area of ministry – on eternal realities, on human mortality, on preparing, in Bunyan's words, to cross the river and teaching us not to be afraid, for we will not be overwhelmed. Some of the most difficult letters I've received have been from those who could not accompany their loved ones in their final hours because of Covid. In the early months of the disease especially, there were moving stories of nurses and doctors taking iPads into the intensive care wards so that the dying and their relatives could have at least some connection in their final hours. I think there is a better understanding now of the need to make that connection as full as we possibly can, and immense care is being taken, especially by our hospital chaplains, to ensure good care in death and bereavement.

What might it mean to take the ordinal at its word? What elements are important in preparing the dying for their death? Why is that a key part of the ministry of a priest? It's a broad subject, but let me offer you five themes which I think need to be reflected in our preparation for death and for dying, whether our own death or the deaths of those close to us.

1   My first is to remember and to know that the experience of death for human beings is universal. We will, all of us, pass through this river. There is no way around it. There is no bridge across it. It is absolutely certain in this life that we will die. We are mortal and, if we are wise, we will live in the knowledge of our mortality. Although, thankfully, in normal times we live in a time and place where there is a generous life expectancy by historical and global averages, life and death are both unpredictable. Our mortality is a gift, on a Christian understanding. Our lives have a fixed term. They do not last forever. That ought to teach us to savour each day, to make the most of each moment, to thank God for every opportunity of grace. Preparing the dying for their death is something which needs to happen through the whole of our lives, not simply at the end.

2   My second is a cry of protest. On a Christian understanding, death is always a bad thing, to be lamented. That is true of our own death and the death of others, especially those we love. There is inevitable sadness and difficulty at the end of any human life. We must not disguise it or overlay it with cheerfulness. Grief is real and very painful. It is a deep part of our humanity to cry out in protest at the fact of our own death or the death of another person. The book of Isaiah, in an earlier section, calls death a shroud which covers all people, a shadow over the whole face of the earth. In the story of the first man and first woman in Genesis 2, death is not an original part of the creation, which God had described as very good; death is a consequence of rebellion against and turning away from God. Death is never something to be finally accepted in Christian theology; although we may find peace and resolution in relation to a particular death, our own or someone else's, some part of us will still rage against the dying of the light.

3   In the tension between these first two points, we find the third part of what it means to prepare for death: to know and understand that

Jesus Christ has conquered death. This is the reason that Bunyan applies Isaiah 43 to every Christian's journey. Jesus Christ gave his life on the cross, a ransom, to use the words of this text. Jesus Christ rose again from the dead on the third day. Christ died so that we might rise with him. Every baptism is a memorial and an anticipation of our death and resurrection as we go down into the waters. Our old self dies with Christ. Our new self rises again with Christ to live abundantly and forever.

Every Eucharist is a memorial of the death and resurrection of Christ. We look back to the gift of his life, his body broken and his blood shed. We look forward in the hope of resurrection to the great banquet in heaven. Every time we celebrate the sacraments of Christ's death and resurrection, we are preparing for life and also preparing for our death.

4   My fourth theme is the call to find and live in the place where we are able to be without fear of death, to live abundantly and fruitfully, accepting our mortality and in confident hope of resurrection. Finding this place, it seems to me, is a continual challenge throughout life. It will mean, certainly in the second half of life, making sure our affairs are in order. There are certain practical tasks it is our responsibility to fulfil in respect of wills, debts, instructions and responsible planning. But there is also our continuous spiritual preparation.

It's instructive to reflect and think about different ways of responding to death in scripture. Simeon is ready to leave this life once he has held the infant Jesus. Christ himself in the garden of Gethsemane has to wrestle with the bitterness of death. Paul and Silas in the prison cell at Philippi are able to sing hymns to God, not knowing what awaits them the next day. Paul, when he writes to the Philippians, draws immense strength and joy from facing his own fear of death and dying:

For to me, living is Christ and dying is gain. If I am to live in the flesh, that means fruitful labour for me; and I do not know which I prefer. I am hard pressed between the two: my desire is to depart and be with Christ, for that is far better; but to remain in the flesh is more necessary for you.

PHILIPPIANS 1:21–24

We may be able to reach an equilibrium with death, and live well. But then something new may disturb us: another phase of our lives; the death of someone we love; the birth of a child and the glimpse of a new future. For many of us, the Covid-19 crisis will have disturbed our security at a deep level, and the fear that has been deep below the waves may have surfaced.

To prepare well for death in the present moment means facing those fears, difficult though they are, and realising ever more deeply the love and the promises of Christ:

> When you pass through the waters, I will be with you;
> and through the rivers, they shall not overwhelm you.

We are to step out of the shadows. We are not to live in fear. If you are not able to find that equilibrium in and of yourself, you are not alone in that. Speak to a church minister. Remember that they are ordained to 'prepare the dying for their death', not simply near the end but all through our lives.

5 And the final part of living with our mortality and preparing well for death is to bear witness in the whole of our lives to the depth of our Christian faith, in our actions and in our words. The world around us is seeking guidance, truth and meaning in response to the most testing season we have known within most of our lifetimes. Those who have

written to me on these themes are absolutely right. The church must not be silent on matters of life, death and eternity when there is so much need of hope. We must gently and graciously invite others to know and cleave to the Lord, whom we know loves them.

Imagine again, if you will, in Bunyan's picture, Christian and Hopeful standing on the bank of the river, facing the flowing waters of death and knowing that they must cross. Hear again, if you will, with that picture in your mind, the profound and life-changing truths of Isaiah 43:

> But now thus says the Lord,
>   he who created you, O Jacob,
>   he who formed you, O Israel:
> Do not fear, for I have redeemed you;
>   I have called you by name, you are mine.
> When you pass through the waters, I will be with you;
>   and through the rivers, they shall not overwhelm you;
> when you walk through fire you shall not be burned
>   and the flame shall not consume you.

6

Will you come and follow me?

– Isaiah 49:1–6 –

Do you ever speculate which songs you would choose if you were a guest on BBC Radio 4's *Desert Island Discs*? One of mine would be 'Sweet Surrender' by John Denver. The song captures for me a sense of love, joy and peace right at the heart of the universe. It played a part in my journey to faith many years ago. It speaks to me of the leading of the Holy Spirit, who illuminates our path and guides us into all truth, enabling us to live without worry as we trust in his guidance.

The comfortable words I want to explore today unfold a mystery at the centre of the universe: that almighty God, maker of heaven and earth, calls women and men into a relationship of love and entrusts us with a purpose for our lives and a mission to God's world.

These are the words of the prophet's song, the second of the four servant songs we will explore:

Listen to me, O coastlands,
    pay attention, you peoples from far away!
The Lord called me before I was born,
    while I was in my mother's womb he named me.
He made my mouth like a sharp sword,
    in the shadow of his hand he hid me;
he made me like a polished arrow,
    in his quiver he hid me away.
And he said to me, 'You are my servant,
    Israel, in whom I will be glorified.'
But I said, 'I have laboured in vain,
    I have spent my strength for nothing and vanity;
yet surely my cause is with the Lord,
    and my reward is with my God.'

And now the Lord says,
    who formed me in the womb to be his servant,
to bring Jacob back to him,
    and that Israel might be gathered to him,
for I am honoured in the sight of the Lord,
    and my God has become my strength –
he says,
'It is too light a thing that you should be my servant
    to raise up the tribes of Jacob
    and to restore the survivors of Israel;
I will give you as a light to the nations,
    that my salvation shall reach to the end of the earth.'
ISAIAH 49:1–6

The prophet is in some ways singing to the nation; as we have seen before, the servant is named as Israel in verse 3. Read in that way, the song evokes the long story of God's dealings with his people, with the call of Abraham and Sarah, Isaac and Rebekah, Jacob and Rachel and Leah. The song also brings a new focus and purpose to that call. The nation Israel is called not for privilege or status but for the sake of the whole world: to be a light to the nations.

But there are many layers of meaning here. The servant is more than a picture or metaphor for the nations. This is one of four passages in Isaiah 40—55 where we are invited to go farther up and farther in. The prophet sings of an individual leader here, one who will come, just as in Isaiah 42:1–4. While this servant will minister to Israel, his ministry will also be to the whole world.

This servant will be known and called before he is born, in his mother's womb. This servant will know suffering and hardship: he will fear that his life's work has been in vain. This servant will be glorified by almighty God and he will become a light to the nations and a means of God's salvation coming to the very ends of the earth.

From earliest times, the church has read this song and the other three servant songs as a prophecy, a vision of the Messiah, fulfilled in the life, ministry, death and resurrection of Jesus Christ.

God's promise, 'I will give you as a light to the nations, that my salvation may reach to the end of the earth', is echoed many times in the New Testament, most famously by Simeon in the temple as he takes the infant Jesus in his arms:

> For my eyes have seen your salvation,
>   which you have prepared in the presence of all peoples,
> a light for revelation to the Gentiles
>   and for glory to your people Israel.
> LUKE 2:30–32

Jesus calls himself 'the light of the world' (John 9:5). Luke quotes this verse again in Acts 13:47, as Barnabas and Paul minister in Antioch of Pisidia and welcome the Gentiles, the nations, into the life of the church. For the Christian, this ancient song about the call of Israel and the call of a leader within Israel becomes a prophecy of the Christ and a frame within which we can understand God's gift to us in Christ.

But the chain of love continues. For we know that God continues in turn to call others in and through Jesus Christ. Jesus in the gospels calls individual people and says to them, 'Follow me.' We are not called to become adherents of a particular religion but disciples of a person: to pattern our lives together on the life of the Son of God. Paul applies these verses not only to Christ but also to the mystery of his own calling: 'God… set me apart before I was born and called me through his grace' (Galatians 1:15).

So the servant's experience of being called by God, set apart from before birth, becomes in every generation the experience of every Christian. The hand of God is upon us. We are all able to say, in Christ, that God made us and knows us, that God knit us together in our mother's womb, to quote the Psalms. We are all able to say that God's invitation comes to all of us to follow. We are all able to say that we have a vocation, a calling, that God invites us to particular tasks and ministries in patterns that unfold throughout our lives, according to our gifts. We will all experience something of the failure, self-questioning and even the suffering of the servant. We are all able to say that those tasks and ministries find their place within God's plan and mission for God's world.

A very important part of being a Christian is the work of discovering God's purpose for our lives, our vocation. The word 'vocation' comes from the Latin *voco*, meaning 'I call'. What is it that God is calling us to do? Vocations sometimes stay constant through our lives; sometimes they change and evolve. Vocations are not just for those called to be clergy, although sometimes the church has used the language of vocation in that way. Vocations are not just for those who serve in church, in youth work or as licensed lay ministers or church officers. God's horizons are on Christ as a light to the entire world, so our vocation is about the whole of what we do and who we are: our everyday faith in our workplace, in our service in the wider community, in our partnerships, in our churches:

> The Lord called me before I was born,
> while I was in my mother's womb he named me.

What is it that God is calling you to be and to do at this stage in your life? What is your calling? How does your life flow and develop from your faith? How is God inviting you to serve God's purposes and mission at this time?

The pandemic has given all of us the opportunity to press the reset button on our lives and to reconsider those deep questions of vocation. That's a matter for personal prayer and discernment, but it's also a really important focus for pastoral conversations.

In the Diocese of Oxford in recent years, we've been developing a way of having more of these conversations and using them to develop personal discipleship plans. Personal discipleship plans are really simple: it's a way of having an encouraging conversation about your everyday faith and about God's call on your life. We don't do that often enough. We've discovered that many Christians can go for many years without the chance simply to explore what God is doing and what the next steps might be.

God calls us. God calls us to service. God calls us as the body of Christ to bring light to the nations, the light of the world who is Jesus. That calling is often challenging. One of the marks of a genuine vocation is that we find it difficult. It will often be messy and frustrating. We will often doubt that we are getting anywhere, just as the servant does in this passage. There will be days when we feel we are in exactly the right place: a sharp sword or an arrow hidden in God's quiver. Then there will be days when we say, 'I have laboured in vain, I have spent my strength for nothing and vanity.' When we are like that, it's time for rest, retreat and encouragement from others; no one can do this on their own.

But there is one more vital lesson for the church today that I want to draw out from this passage. The servant is called from birth and from before birth. Twice in six verses we find references to his mother's womb:

The Lord called me before I was born,
    while I was in my mother's womb he named me.
ISAIAH 49:2

And now the Lord says,
    who formed me in the womb to be his servant.
ISAIAH 49:5

God's call to the servant comes even before the servant is born. As with Samuel, David and Jeremiah in the Old Testament, like Mary, Jesus, John the Baptist and Paul in the New Testament, God's call comes to those who are very young.

As we read these words today, our thoughts, prayers and imagination should be drawn to God's call to children and young people today. God's call is coming to them.

We still don't know, of course, the ultimate impact of the Covid pandemic on the church. As I look and listen across the diocese, there are many encouraging signs of life and health, although there is much that is difficult. One of the most demanding areas of our life to reset and rebuild will be our ministry to children, young people and families.

There is much that is good still happening, thanks to the hard work, dedication and skill of youth and children's workers and many hundreds of volunteers. But there is much still to do. There need to be some key shifts in the way the church reimagines our ministry with children, young people and families. They are all supported by the insights of Isaiah 49.

We are called to view children and young people as active participants and pilgrims – fellow Christians and part of the church today, not the church of tomorrow.

We are to engage with children and young people intergenerationally – not simply run separate programmes at separate times.

We are to be intentional disciple-makers, to help children and young people listen to and grow into the call God makes on their lives.

We are to support, form and honour those whose primary calling is to do ministry with children, young people and families. We are not so much looking for volunteers as those who sense a vocation to this work.

And we are to try to be the change we want to see. We are never called to be an adults-only church, but an all-age community of grace.

If we are to take this particular servant song seriously, we will be alert to the gifts and skills that children, young people and families bring to the resetting and rebuilding of the church through lockdown and after lockdown. We will already be making space in our planning meetings and our ministries for children and young people to offer their gifts. We will be seeking to listen to everyone as we rebuild for the future, because all are called in every way to be a part of God's church and God's kingdom.

> It is too light a thing that you should be my servant
>> to raise up the tribes of Jacob
>> and to restore the survivors of Israel;
> I will give you as a light to the nations,
>> that my salvation shall reach to the end of the earth.

The world can be a dark place. There is fear and confusion all around us. Jesus fulfils the promise of these verses when he makes the astounding claim, 'I am the light of the world.' Jesus Christ is the servant at the heart of these songs, and these songs in turn shape the church's understanding of what that means in every generation. It is a big, cosmic, universal claim. Christ is not just for us and for people like us but for the whole world.

But Jesus also says to the tiny group of disciples who gather around him for the sermon on the mount, 'You are the light of the world' (Matthew 5:14). This extraordinary prophecy in Isaiah 49 finds part of its fulfilment in every generation in the church – in families, children, young people and adult disciples living out our everyday faith.

7

A word for the weary

– Isaiah 50:4–9 –

The title for this book, *Comfortable Words*, comes from two different places. The first is the opening song of this prophet, 'Comfort, O comfort my people' (Isaiah 40:1). The second is the phrase used in the Book of Common Prayer for a particular group of texts: the comfortable words.

These words are spoken by the priest at the centre of the service of Holy Communion. After we have confessed our sins, the priest says, 'Hear what comfortable words our Saviour Christ says to all who truly turn to him.' There are then three scripture verses, the first of which is:

Come unto me, all ye that travail and are heavy laden, and I will refresh you.
MATTHEW 11:28 (Book of Common Prayer)

The world, our country and our church stand in need of great comfort as we move forward in a post-Covid world. All of the challenges facing the world before the coronavirus pandemic are still present, but most of them are now heightened. There is real inequality, a sharper challenge to care for the earth and a need to grapple with the challenges of new technology.

Many of us are already weary from all that we have been carrying. We stand in great need of these comfortable words ourselves, and so do the communities we serve.

We've not been this way before, and there is little to guide us. But perhaps we might start with that old English word, 'comfort'. Its meaning has changed a little from the meaning we find in the scriptures. Today, comfort is something soft, like a big hug, soothing us, enfolding us. It is also a well-known fabric conditioner, but that's not the whole story.

Comfort can be gentle and tender, certainly, and it has love at its heart, but that's not the core meaning in Isaiah or in the Book of Common Prayer. The English word 'comfort' comes from two Latin words: *com*, meaning with, and *fortis*, meaning strength – and from which we also derive the word 'fortitude', meaning bravery. So to comfort someone is not simply to wrap them up with cotton wool and tenderness. Comfortable words are words that restore our strength, our core, our backbone; words that give us energy to stand our ground and move forward; words that helped the exiles find the courage and the character to leave Babylon and rebuild their city and their country, exactly the task which lies before us now and in the coming years.

As the world emerges from the virus, we have to find the resources, somehow, to give strength to our families and communities when we are already tired and worn down by disease, fear and grief. The days ahead will test our faith. We will need to draw on the deepest wells we can find in one of the greatest challenges of our lives and of our life as a church. With all my heart I want to say to you: have the courage in this time to go deeper into God and deeper into your faith and draw on the great reservoirs of courage God gives to his people in these seasons.

One of those deep wells is the passage we come to this week. This is the third of the four great servant songs in Isaiah 40—55. The prophet sings of the leadership that is required in times of great crisis, not just for the exiles but in every generation. The prophet sings as well of the leader, God's anointed, who will come. Each of these songs points forward to Jesus, God's Messiah. The prophet sings of the leadership the followers of Jesus are called to exercise in every generation.

The first part of the song speaks of the way in which the servant's ministry is rooted for this time of crisis in teaching, listening and a willingness to bear hardship and suffering:

> The Lord God has given me
> the tongue of a teacher,
> that I may know how to sustain
> the weary with a word.
> Morning by morning he wakens –
> wakens my ear
> to listen as those who are taught.
> The Lord God has opened my ear,
> and I was not rebellious,
> I did not turn backwards.
> I gave my back to those who struck me,
> and my cheeks to those who pulled out the beard;
> I did not hide my face
> from insult and spitting.
> ISAIAH 50:4–6

Four times in this song we find the phrase, 'The Lord God'. Each time the phrase is followed by a strong verb, something God is doing. The ministry of the servant is God's doing and God's calling. The servant is responding all the time to God's actions.

- 'The Lord God has given me the tongue of a teacher' (v. 4)
- 'The Lord God has opened my ear' (v. 5)
- 'The Lord God helps me' (v. 7)
- 'It is the Lord God who helps me' (v. 9)

To draw comfort and strength from the song, we may need first a change of perspective. The ministry we are called to exercise is not ours but God's. This is God's world and God's church. We are called to discover what God is doing and what God would have us do to join in. All too easily in times of crisis, we try to take the whole world on our shoulders – but as we do that, so the weight of everything will crush us. So remember to pass that burden back to God, the maker and creator. Then be ready to take up the part, to offer the help, that God asks of you and that no one else can give.

As we have seen with the other servant songs, these words of the prophet are fulfilled in a particular way in Jesus. He is the one, supremely, whom God has called to be a teacher, a rabbi, able to find the right word for every situation, the one who tells the best stories, the one who crafts the most memorable sayings and the one who draws the crowds with his parables and images. And Jesus is the one who morning by morning in his earthly ministry draws near to God and listens, who spends time alone with his Father, who does nothing that he does not see the Father doing.

Although the words apply to Christ first and foremost, they also set the pattern for everyone who follows him. We too are called to this service, and our service to a weary world needs to begin exactly where the servant's ministry begins, with listening to God. That listening is to be a daily discipline:

> Morning by morning he wakens –
>   wakens my ear
>   to listen as those who are taught.
> The Lord God has opened my ear.

Notice the repetition: 'Morning by morning'; 'he wakens – wakens'; 'my ear… my ear'.

I once heard a talk which offered the very attractive translation 'morning by morning he digs out my ears', to emphasise how difficult it is to listen to God and how many things get in the way. Sadly, I can find no support in the Hebrew for that translation, but it's a great concept.

But the original does imply that God needs to wake up our ears every day to listen to a fresh word for that day: give us this day our daily spiritual bread. And the original says clearly that God needs to open our ears, as Jesus opens the ears of the deaf, to hear what God is saying to us every single morning of our lives.

The message is very clear and very simple: if we are to serve God well in these times, we will need to give a first priority, early in the morning when the world is still, to allow God to open our ears to what God is saying, to find and discover a word for that day, the word that will sustain the weary around us. Listening to God and to this weary world is the first keystone of the servant's ministry in giving comfort.

The second, which we are also to imitate, is strength and resilience. The word we hear and the word we are called to bring may not be welcome. Already in the first half of the song, we are introduced to the suffering of the servant:

I gave my back to those who struck me,
    and my cheeks to those who pulled out the beard;
I did not hide my face
    from insult and spitting.

The words are echoed in the gospels, such as Matthew 26:67 and 27:30, which describe the trial and crucifixion of Jesus, the suffering servant of God who fulfils these prophecies.

The second half of the song has more on this theme and another striking image for a part of the body:

> The Lord God helps me;
>   therefore I have not been disgraced;
> therefore I have set my face like flint,
>   and I know that I shall not be put to shame;
>   he who vindicates me is near.
> ISAIAH 50:7–8

The servant is going to have to persevere through suffering and difficulty. The words the servant brings will be life for some but resisted by others. The prophet to the exiles would have experienced persecution from Babylon but also pushback from his own people, who may have settled too well in a strange land and not wanted to return. To comfort the disturbed will often mean disturbing those who are comfortable.

Jesus experienced resistance and persecution in the same way both from the Roman governors of Judea and from his own people – and sometimes from his own disciples and followers.

Are we to crumple and fold in the face of resistance and opposition? By no means. The song deploys the image first used by Ezekiel, who was called to deliver a difficult message to a rebellious house. God says to Ezekiel:

> Like the hardest stone, harder than flint, I have made your forehead;
> do not fear them or be dismayed at their looks, for they are a rebel-
> lious house.
> EZEKIEL 3:9

Ezekiel has to deliver a message of judgement. We might think that a message of hope – good news – would not call for the same steel. But that is not the case for Isaiah's servant, nor for Jesus. Luke tells us that at a certain point in his ministry, Jesus set his face to go to Jerusalem (Luke 9:51). This is a turning point in the gospel story, and I think an echo of this verse in Isaiah. Both Jesus and the servant are called to set their faces like flint, even as they deliver words that can bring healing. And so are we.

When I became a bishop in 2009, one of the things I had to do was choose a ring: part of the episcopal kit. Most bishops' rings are quite ornate and have a precious stone set in, normally, gold. They are a sign of the bishop's love for and commitment to the church, the bride of Christ, and especially to the diocese.

I struggled with having to choose and wear an episcopal ring, but eventually I chose a simple steel band with no stone. That was inspired in part by Sheffield, where I was first called to be bishop, a city built on forging metal in the crucible, especially steel. But it was inspired also by my needing a symbol of determination and resilience. I'm not always able to live up to it, but the ring has been a sign to me of the commitment of love at the heart of my calling. Because God stands by me and for me, I have, at least some of the time, the strength and determination to keep going. We all need that flint, that steel, in our discipleship in the present times.

We will hear more in the longest and deepest of the servant songs about the suffering of the servant and the deep redemptive purpose of that suffering. But here we need to ask the question: where exactly is the comfort in this call to become rock-like in our commitment and dedication, to set our faces like flint? It's certainly not the comfort of a warm embrace. There is nothing fluffy about this kind of call.

There is, however, comfort in the ancient sense of the word: we draw great strength from being men and women of depth and conviction in these times, people who stand by our post, who are determined to dig in, dig deep and keep on loving and living well.

I hope and pray that the church that emerges from the pandemic will be a church that mirrors the qualities of the servant in this ancient song, the qualities of Christ.

I hope we will be a church characterised by humility, a servant church.

I hope we will be a church characterised by listening to God and being able to speak the words that will sustain the weary around us.

And I hope we will be a resilient church, able to set our faces like flint, determined to bear witness to the way of love in the midst of all the suffering around us. Peter was called to be like rock – and so are we. In this spirit of being rock-like, perhaps everyone needs to be a little boulder. It's a terrible pun, but irresistible.

Finally, it's always interesting to see where the insights of the deep well of scripture surface in the contemporary world. One of my favourite secular books on leadership is *Good to Great* by Jim Collins (Harper, 2001). The book is a study of the elements that enable the building of great companies that can sustain growth not just over a few years but over decades. Collins extended his work to other kinds of organisations in *Good to Great and the Social Sectors* (Random House, 2006).

According to Collins, one of the key factors in developing great organisations is a particular kind of leadership – what he calls 'level 5 leadership' – that goes beyond skills and knowledge to two vital qualities of character: personal humility and professional will.

These two vital qualities are exactly the qualities evidenced in Isaiah 50:4–9. Leaders are servants first, with the humility to listen both to God and to others, daily. But they are resilient and determined, not for themselves but to fulfil their mission.

This is exactly the kind of leadership that is needed now in families, schools and workplaces, in charities and hospitals, in universities and churches. It's exactly the leadership we need in local and national government.

This is the leadership which brings comfort, strength and hope in times of immense difficulty.

> The Lord God has given me
>   the tongue of a teacher,
> that I may know how to sustain
>   the weary with a word.
> Morning by morning he wakens –
>   wakens my ear
>   to listen as those who are taught…
> The Lord God helps me;
>   therefore I have not been disgraced;
> therefore I have set my face like flint,
>   and I know that I shall not be put to shame;
>   he who vindicates me is near.

May God bless you in your service, your listening and your determination and courage.

Lamb of God

– Isaiah 52:13—53:12 –

In services of Holy Communion all over the world, at the most solemn moment in the service, the priest breaks the consecrated bread and these words are said or sung:

> Lamb of God, you take away the sin of the world; have mercy upon us.
> Lamb of God, you take away the sin of the world; have mercy upon us.
> Lamb of God, you take away the sin of the world; grant us peace.

The priest and the people then receive the bread and wine. The words are a cry for help and forgiveness as we come with empty hands to receive the grace of God and to begin our lives again, Sunday by Sunday.

The use of these words in the liturgy is very ancient. The words themselves are taken in part from the gospel of John, where John the Baptist sees Jesus coming towards him and declares:

> Here is the Lamb of God who takes away the sin of the world!
> JOHN 1:29

But the words echo the most famous song of our unnamed prophet who sang to the exiles in Babylon more than 500 years before the birth of Christ. This prophet has given us so many comfortable words: songs that have given strength and hope to the people of God across the generations and across the world in seasons of immense difficulty, like this one.

The people to whom the prophet sings stand at the crossroads. As the end of their exile approaches, will they find the resources to stand again, journey back to Jerusalem and rebuild their nation to keep alive the promise to Abraham, the gift of the law through Moses and the testimony of the prophets to the peace and justice of God? Will they be able to come to terms with their own failure as a nation and hear these words of forgiveness and tenderness? Will they be able to respond to God's call to be a light to the nations?

Three times now the prophet has sung to us so beautifully of the servant of God:

1 the servant will be gentle – he will not break a bruised reed or quench a dimly burning wick (Isaiah 42:1–9)
2 the servant's mission is not to Israel alone but to the whole world – a light to the nations (Isaiah 49:1–6)
3 the servant understands how to sustain the weary, yet has to set his face like flint in the face of his own suffering (Isaiah 50:4–9).

The fourth song begins at Isaiah 52:13 and runs through to 53:12. This is the longest of the four servant songs as well as the most graphic and the most personal; it is the suffering of the servant which takes centre stage here.

At one level, the song is a reflection on the suffering of the nation and the way God will raise up his people again, no matter how difficult the circumstances or how far they have fallen.

But as Christians have read these words, from the very beginning of the church, we have been inspired to see far more than this in the prophet's words. This is a profound reflection on the servant of God who is to come, God's anointed. The song describes the kind of leader, the nature of the king whom God will send. The song unfolds the nature of the servant's mission and the meaning of his suffering.

The book of Acts tells the story of a eunuch from Ethiopia, travelling home by chariot from a visit to Jerusalem and to the temple there. This eunuch has a longing for God, but because of his disfigurement and the fact that he is a Gentile, he will have learned that he can never belong fully to the people of God. As he travels, the eunuch is reading aloud from Isaiah 53:

> Like a sheep he was led to the slaughter,
>   and like a lamb silent before its shearer,
>   so he does not open his mouth.
> ACTS 8:32 quoting ISAIAH 53:7

By a miracle of God, by the guidance of the Spirit, Philip the Evangelist draws alongside this seeker and, starting with this scripture, proclaims the good news about Jesus. The eunuch discovers that, after all, whatever his race, background and sexuality, he is acceptable to God. He stops the chariot and is baptised and becomes a member of the church, the first Gentile to do so according to the Acts narrative.

In another well-known passage at the end of Luke's gospel, two disciples are walking to a place called Emmaus on the first Easter Day. The risen Jesus falls into step with them, walking in the wrong direction. Jesus is giving priority to finding the lost sheep, the ones who are wandering away from the community in Jerusalem. Jesus listens to them – to their hurt, grief and questions – and then he says to them:

'Was it not necessary that the Messiah should suffer these things and then enter into his glory?' Then beginning with Moses and all the prophets, he interpreted to them the things concerning himself in all the scriptures.

LUKE 24:26–27

We don't know exactly where Jesus began his exposition of the scriptures, but there is a strong tradition that this song in Isaiah 53 formed his starting point: it was necessary for the Messiah to suffer these things and enter his glory. The prophet of the exile sees and captures in this song the mystery of the suffering of the servant of the Lord and its meaning for every generation.

The disciples are expecting a messiah who will come as conqueror to bring an earthly kingdom. This is part of the narrative of the scriptures. But there is a deeper story. Jesus comes to take upon himself the suffering and sin of the world and to give his life to establish the kingdom of heaven. God raises him to glory.

Early in the song are words that many have seen as describing the earthly life of Jesus, an unknown carpenter from an obscure village in Galilee:

> He was despised and rejected by others;
>   a man of suffering and acquainted with infirmity;
> and as one from whom others hide their faces
>   he was despised, and we held him of no account.
> ISAIAH 53:3

God comes in Jesus not to the wealthy and powerful nor to the secure and outwardly beautiful, but to lepers, tax collectors and sex workers and to the maimed, the chronically sick and the poor – the people who stand in the margins, who are overlooked.

The singer Gregory Porter has a beautiful song, 'Take Me to the Alley', which captures this profound good news that the Son of God stands with the rejected and overlooked:

> Take me to the alley, take me to the afflicted ones,
> Take me to the lonely ones that somehow lost their way.
> Let them hear me say
> I am your friend. Come to my table. Rest here in my garden. You will
>   have a pardon.

This is the message of Isaiah 53: that Christ stands with, for and as the neglected. This is good news for people who have reached the end of their own resources, who are weary, wounded and exhausted, who know they cannot get up by themselves, who know that they have failed. It is therefore good news for us in this place now. We have to depend on the grace of God. But there is more.

The servant comes not to reign, but to suffer, and his suffering is to have a particular and profound meaning:

> Surely he has borne our infirmities
>   and carried our diseases;
> yet we accounted him stricken,
>   struck down by God, and afflicted.
> But he was wounded for our transgressions,
>   crushed for our iniquities;
> upon him was the punishment that made us whole,
>   and by his bruises we are healed.
> ISAIAH 53:4–5

This is a profound and powerful mystery at the heart of our faith. Jesus stands with and for the poor and despised, but his gift is more than solidarity. Jesus endures profound suffering: he is despised, rejected and spat upon; though innocent, he is condemned to death; he is betrayed and abandoned by his friends; he is flogged, beaten and crucified.

The prophet's song sets out clearly that all of this undeserved suffering has a purpose even greater than God's identification with the abandoned. This suffering is intended to bring forgiveness and healing without limit and measure. The forgiveness and healing are for all. The forgiveness and healing are for us.

We can never come to the end of understanding how there is forgiveness and healing through the suffering and death of Jesus Christ. The whole of scripture bears witness to this and helps us explore how this forgiveness happens. The church has been reflecting for 2,000 years on the mystery of God's goodness to us in Christ. Thankfully we do not need to understand this gift. We are simply invited to receive it.

The prophet goes on to say:

> He was oppressed, and he was afflicted,
>   yet he did not open his mouth;
> Like a lamb that is led to the slaughter
>   and like a sheep that before its shearers is silent,
>   so he did not open his mouth.
> ISAIAH 53:7

This is the interpretation of his death that Jesus himself gives to his disciples. This is what we remember in every celebration of Holy Communion. In Matthew's account we read this:

> While they were eating, Jesus took a loaf of bread, and after blessing it he broke it, gave it to the disciples and said, 'Take, eat; this is my

body.' Then he took a cup, and after giving thanks he gave it to them, saying, 'Drink from it, all of you; for this is my blood of the covenant, which is poured out for many for the forgiveness of sins.'
MATTHEW 26:26–28

The prophet sings of the identification of the servant with the lost, the last and the least. The prophet sings of the redemptive meaning of his suffering: the servant becomes the sacrifice, the lamb of God who takes away the sin of the world, in John the Baptist's words.

But if this were not enough, the prophet is given a third and even deeper insight into the mystery of God's purposes. The servant is to suffer and suffer greatly – even to death. But this is not the whole story. The servant's suffering is set in the context of his exaltation and his glory.

This is perhaps the deepest mystery of this fourth servant song. The prophet does not cast this song as a psalm of lament. The song is cast, rather, as a song of thanksgiving. This is how it begins:

> See, my servant shall prosper;
>   he shall be exalted and lifted up
>   and shall be very high.
> ISAIAH 52:13

And this is how the song ends, in testimony to God's grace in lifting up the servant:

> The righteous one, my servant, shall make many righteous
>   and he shall bear their iniquities.
> Therefore I will allot him a portion with the great,
>   and he shall divide the spoil with the strong;

because he poured out himself to death,
    and was numbered with the transgressors;
yet he bore the sin of many,
    and made intercession for the transgressors.
ISAIAH 53:11–12

Isaiah reaches forward here, seeing through a glass darkly, but still seeing, in the words of Jesus on the Emmaus Road, that it was 'necessary that the Messiah should suffer these things and then enter into his glory'.

The fourth servant song is one of the highest mountaintops of scripture, a passage which draws together the deep insights of the theologians of the exile into the purposes of God and of human suffering; a passage on which the writers of the New Testament draw over and over again as they seek to understand their encounters with Jesus Christ in his earthly ministry, in his death and resurrection and in the worshipping life of the church.

How are we to hear these words today afresh, as we reassess our lives, the life of the church and the life of the nation? Let me offer you three reflections.

1   The first is to return again to the centre of our faith. The forgiveness we seek and need is freely available through faith and is without limit. But also remember that this forgiveness was won at great cost – the cost of the faithful witness of the people of God, before the coming of Jesus, to God's truth and justice; the witness of the Christian church down the centuries and of those who have given their lives to bear witness to the gospel; but most of all the love and the passion of Christ himself, who endured suffering, who fulfilled his mission and who walked the way of the cross, so that we and all the world might receive healing and forgiveness in this world and the next.

The experience of this terrible pandemic will, I hope, help us to revalue much of what we have taken for granted: the ability to embrace a friend, to mingle with crowds, to go out for the evening, to travel, to see our families. In all of that revaluing, I hope that all Christians will return to a deeper appreciation of our faith and of the suffering and resurrection of Christ at its centre.

2 The second is to be reminded of our baptism. When he has understood this passage fully, the Ethiopian eunuch in his chariot knows that, at last, through Jesus Christ, whatever his background, he is able to belong to the people of God. He stops the chariot and cries out, 'Look, here is water! What is to prevent me from being baptised?' (Acts 8:37).

I hope and pray that understanding this passage afresh may lead some to seek baptism for the first time: to know and understand that you are part of the people of God, that you belong. I hope and pray that others will be drawn from baptism to confirmation – to an adult declaration of faith and a prayer to be filled with God's Holy Spirit. I pray that all of us will understand more fully the value of our own baptism: that we have identified with the death and resurrection of Jesus and that we might offer that gift to others.

3 Third, and finally, in the midst of so much that is difficult, I hope and pray that we will be reminded of the need to persevere. The letter to the Hebrews is written to Christians who have suffered a great deal for their faith. The letter unfolds to them in many and various ways, over and over again, the wonder of the gospel and of their salvation. This is how Hebrews sums up the lessons of this journey:

> Let us hold fast to the confession of our hope without wavering, for he who has promised is faithful. And let us consider how to pro-voke one another to love and good deeds, not neglecting to meet

together, as is the habit of some, but encouraging one another, and all the more as you see the Day approaching.

HEBREWS 10:23–25

May God give us grace to receive his love, healing and forgiveness in Jesus Christ and to encourage one another in this journey.

Come to the waters

– Isaiah 55 –

We've been travelling together with the unknown prophet who has given us a series of beautiful songs to guide us and strengthen us in this time of trial.

The songs were first sung to the exiles in Babylon over 500 years before the birth of Christ. God was calling his people to make the long journey home again to Jerusalem. They were called to leave the captivity, but also the comforts, of Babylon. Before they could go, the prophet needed to comfort God's people, to give them hope and strength again, to gather them together, to remind them of the leadership they would need. Above all, the prophet sang to let the people know that they were forgiven people with a vital message of light and life for the whole world.

In every generation, for 2,500 years, God's people have listened to the prophet's songs to find inspiration, hope and strength in troubled times. These are lyrics that have shaped the world and the church. We've turned them into hymns and songs of our own in different styles. They are like a rich, underground stream that goes on feeding us even when the ground is dry.

And so we come now to this final chapter, Isaiah 55, which is meant to be read as one continuous piece and ends this part of the book of Isaiah. The final eleven chapters of Isaiah relate more to the time after the return and the challenges of learning to live again in Jerusalem. This chapter is about comings and goings, and it sets a profound rhythm for the life of God's people – a rhythm that flows through the New Testament and through the worship of the church.

The first verses of Isaiah 55 offer the most gracious and powerful invitation for thirsty, weary souls:

> Ho, everyone who thirsts,
>   come to the waters;
> and you that have no money,
>   come, buy and eat!
> Come, buy wine and milk
>   without money and without price.
> ISAIAH 55:1

There is an echo here of a beautiful image in Proverbs, where Wisdom lays the table, sets the feast and issues an invitation:

> Come, eat of my bread
>   and drink of the wine I have mixed.
> PROVERBS 9:5

But our prophet turns this into a fuller and deeper invitation still.

To begin with, the speaker in Isaiah 55 is not Wisdom personified but almighty God, the maker of heaven and earth. After the pain and the difficulty of exile, after all the suffering, guilt, doubt and despair, God is drawing near. God comes to a place where we can meet together. This is profound and wonderful good news.

Second, this invitation is to those who have come to the end of their own resources, who have nothing, who know that they are poor in spirit. This invitation is to those who know not only their need of God, but also that they have nothing to bring in return.

One of the best-known hymns in the entire world is 'Amazing Grace'. The hymn was first sung in the parish of Olney, part of the diocese of Oxford, on 1 January 1773. It was written by the curate at the time, John Newton, a former slave trader, to illustrate a sermon. I recently received a lovely invitation from the present vicar of Olney to visit the parish for the celebrations to mark 250 years since the first singing of the hymn. 'Amazing Grace' has spoken to millions of people all across the world. Newton's words echo this theme of Isaiah 55, that we come with nothing:

> Amazing grace, how sweet the sound
> That saved a wretch like me
> I once was lost, but now am found;
> Was blind, but now I see.

In Isaiah 55, almighty God comes to us, spreads a table of good things before us and invites us to come and drink and to eat without money and without price. There are no conditions here.

A third profound difference from the invitation in Proverbs is that it is God himself who is our food, our sustenance and our purpose. In Proverbs 9, Wisdom invites us to attend to her teaching. That is part of the meaning in Isaiah 55, certainly – we are invited to 'listen carefully' (v. 2) and to 'incline your ear' (v. 3). But what is this good, rich food that satisfies and that is the true bread? The answer comes in verse 6, a second invitation to come:

> Seek the Lord while he may be found,
> call upon him while he is near.

We are invited to a dinner. The invitation has been given by God, who comes to meet us and spreads a table for us. The invitation is given to all who are thirsty, all who are weary. There is no entrance fee. There are no qualifications needed. The food at the banquet is not simply guidance or teaching for our lives. The food at the banquet is the person who invites us: the Lord himself. He is the true bread. He is the rich food which satisfies. He is the one who gives life.

These are the words of Jesus, again using our prophet's song as a springboard and inspiration:

> I am the bread of life. Whoever comes to me will never be hungry, and whoever believes in me will never be thirsty.
> JOHN 6:35

And later:

> I am the living bread that came down from heaven.
> JOHN 6:51

God draws near and invites us to come into this mystical fellowship and friendship, this relationship with our maker, offered freely and without price. God makes that offer to all who are hungry, thirsty, weary and heavy laden. God makes that offer to us.

The later verses of the song make it very clear that the prophet is not diluting or taming our understanding of God. We are reminded, as we have been reminded in earlier songs, that this really is the maker of the heavens and the earth:

For my thoughts are not your thoughts,
    nor are your ways my ways, says the Lord.
For as the heavens are higher than the earth,
    so are my ways higher than your ways
    and my thoughts than your thoughts.
ISAIAH 55:8–9

We are reminded as well that the way we begin to draw near to God is to listen to God's word, the word by which God created the heavens and the earth, the words the prophets speak. This is why, morning by morning, he opens our ears, so that we can hear the word of life. But undoubtedly the word is given to show us the majesty, grace and fullness of God. In the full Christian understanding, God's written word points forward to God's living word, God's Son Jesus Christ, who comes to us, the fulfilment of the songs of the servant. Jesus draws near to us and invites his disciples to come and see, to follow. Jesus gives his life to open up the way for us to come to God. Jesus is himself the bread of life, the living bread, to whom we come daily to be resourced for this life's journey and to share in the life to come.

So the prophet almost ends this collection of comfortable words with this invitation to come, to return to the Lord. It's an invitation we need to hear as we look forward to the end of our own exile, of our lockdown; as we look forward, God willing, to Pentecost and to the end of more than a year of confinement and lockdown with all that has meant. Wherever you are, whoever you are, we all need to hear God's gracious invitation to us: 'Come to the waters.'

The prophet almost ends their collection there – but not quite. For there is one final chorus, and in that chorus the invitation to come in is balanced by an invitation to go out:

You shall go out with joy,
>   and be led back in peace;
the mountains and the hills before you
>   shall burst into song,
>   and all the trees of the field shall clap their hands.
ISAIAH 55:12

In its context, this is a tremendous song of hope, joy and return from exile. But the prophet also unfolds for us what it means to be a disciple and to know God. We do not live in a one-sided rhythm of simply coming and receiving. The Christian life is not simply about being fed and nourished by God. Our Christian life is about coming together so that we can then go out, with joy and in love and service to the world.

The earliest description of the call of the disciples in the New Testament is in Mark's gospel:

[Jesus] went up the mountain and called to him those whom he wanted, and they came to him. And he appointed twelve, whom he also named apostles.
MARK 3:13–14

This is a solemn moment. Jesus is creating the foundations of the new Israel. There are twelve, because of the twelve tribes. What we are about to read is not simply a statement about the first group of disciples but about the church in every generation. What did Jesus call the disciples for?

And he appointed twelve, whom he also named apostles, to be with him, and to be sent out.

'To be with him, and to be sent out' – this is the rhythm at the heart of the Christian life into which Christ invites us. We are to come and eat the bread that satisfies. We are to go out with joy and live our lives to the glory of God. This is the rhythm we see in the life of the disciples in the gospels and in Acts. They draw together to be with Jesus in the time of his earthly ministry and in the time after the resurrection and Pentecost. In that drawing together they are nourished and strengthened. Then they are sent out again with joy to serve and to witness.

The same rhythm is present in our Lord's great summary of the law: we are to love the Lord our God with all our heart, soul, mind and strength and also to love our neighbours as ourselves (see Mark 12:30–31). We draw together with the living God to express that love and adoration and to nurture our relationship with God. We go out to celebrate all that this life means and to dedicate our lives in love and service to our God.

All of this reflection on meals and on comings and goings and the rhythm of our lives brings us to the Eucharist, the sacrament at the heart of our life as Christians, the worship that Jesus commands his church to do. When we come together, we are to do this in remembrance of him.

The Eucharist is a meal after the pattern of Isaiah 55. We come with empty hands. We come hungry and thirsty to hear words of life and for food that will nourish and satisfy. We come for God himself.

We come to listen with care to the word of God read and interpreted: the word which brings life, which is like seed planted in our hearts, the creative word which never returns to the sender empty.

We gather as the disciples of Jesus to be with Jesus together. We remember his ministry as a servant and his suffering, death and resurrection and all they bring to us and all they mean. At the heart of our worship, we come together and, in normal times, we eat bread and drink wine, doing so in remembrance of him. We enjoy and we appreciate this Holy Communion, this fellowship with Jesus in this most holy space and time. We thank God for this grace, which is given to us.

But all of this is for a reason. We are called so that we can be sent. We come so that we are then able to go and to go out with joy. We offer our lives again in response to God's grace to us and then at the end of the service we are sent out in service: 'Go in peace to love and serve the Lord. In the name of Christ. Amen.'

We are the people of God, missionary disciples, called and sent, living in the rhythm of Isaiah 55, coming together to be with Jesus and sent out to serve him with joy in God's world.

One of the hardest parts of the lockdown periods for many Christians has been absence from in-person worship and especially from receiving the sacraments, in particular the Eucharist. It has been acutely painful not to be able to live in these deep rhythms of the Christian life: not to be able without a second thought to come to the church, to kneel and confess our sins, to receive assurance of forgiveness, to listen to God's word in familiar places and to sing God's praises, to hold and touch our fellow pilgrims, to gather around the table of the Lord, to receive bread and wine, to enjoy Holy Communion with our God, to be sent out again to live with joy.

God is with us and we have learned many lessons, but there is also, for many, a sense of exile, especially from the Eucharist, receiving bread and wine as God's people.

As we start to regather as churches and as life begins to return to some kind of normality, we need to notice the things we have really missed that sustain our spiritual journey – and especially to notice how hard it has been not to gather around the table of the Lord in person and to share in bread and wine. In that noticing, it would be easy to let the pain we have experienced turn into resentment against this or that person, or even against God. Try not to go in that direction. Instead turn this sense of missing the Eucharist into a deeper longing to return to God, to enjoy and appreciate the sacraments in a fuller and more disciplined way, through a desire to be more regularly present when that becomes possible, through more careful devotional preparation, through extending and deepening your understanding of what Christ has done for us.

This final song of our unknown prophet is one of the deepest of the comfortable words, for it sets the pattern for our whole lifetime: a pattern of comings and goings. We are forever invited to come to the waters, to the table of the Lord, to be refreshed and made new and to find food that satisfies. We are forever invited to go out with joy and to bear witness to the grace we have seen in lives of service and in our testimony to God's love and grace.

And finally...

Thanks for making the journey. The prophet's songs have helped us to explore songs of comfort, acknowledge our own weariness, reflect on the leadership we offer, explore our attitudes to suffering and death and, most of all, reflect on Jesus Christ, his nature and calling and the way his incarnation, ministry, death and resurrection are 'according to the scriptures'.

The destruction of Jerusalem by the armies of Babylon in 587BC was a seminal event in the history of Israel and therefore in the history of the world. It took the people of Judah, those in exile and those who remained in Jerusalem, generations to work through the tragedy and trauma of those years. Much of what we now know of as the Old Testament was collected and formed in this 70-year period, as the prophets, sages and teachers drew on the earlier history of God's people and wrestled with their own failures.

The different groups developed very different responses to help people understand what had happened, which we can still find within Israel's history books and in the writings of Jeremiah and Ezekiel. The nation had many trials and tribulations ahead still, after the return began.

But the songs of Isaiah 40—55 are a high point in that story, drawing us into God's love for the world and for God's people, bringing us hope for the future and pointing us always towards the servant leader who will come, whom the gospel writers recognise in Jesus Christ.

Navigating through the post-Covid world will not be the work of a few weeks or months. It will take many years to come to terms with what has happened, to grieve for those who have died, to rebuild the economy of the world and, hopefully, to learn how to reset our societies in line with the vision of the kingdom of God we find in the whole book of Isaiah.

As we engage with that task and live through these years, we will need to return to deep springs and wells of life, to come to the waters, in the words of Isaiah 55, again and again to be nourished and fed and to find again these comfortable words.

May God bless you in that task and in this journey.

Deep Calls to Deep

Spiritual formation
in the hard places of life

Tony Horsfall

The Psalms offer honest insights into the reality of life with God, reflecting every human emotion and situation. Through looking at some of the psalms written 'from the depths', we can understand more fully the way in which God is at work to shape our characters and form the life of Christ within us during difficult times. *Deep Calls to Deep* speaks to those who are 'passing through the valley'. It will also be helpful to anyone who desires a deeper walk with God, as well as those who accompany others on their Christian journey as mentors, soul friends or spiritual directors.

Deep Calls to Deep
Spiritual formation in the hard places of life
Tony Horsfall
978 1 80039 066 9 £8.99

brfonline.org.uk

Servant Ministry
A portrait of Christ and a pattern for his followers
Tony Horsfall

Servant Ministry offers a practical exposition of the first 'Servant Song' in Isaiah (42:1–9). Writing from many years of Christian teaching and mentoring, Tony Horsfall applies insights drawn from the Isaiah passage to topics such as the motivation for service and the call to serve; valid expressions of servanthood and the link between evangelism and social action; character formation and what it means to be a servant; how to keep going over the long haul in the harsh realities of ministry; the importance of listening to God on a daily basis and also over a whole lifetime.

Servant Ministry
A portrait of Christ and a pattern for his followers
Tony Horsfall
978 0 85746 886 4 £8.99

brfonline.org.uk

MAY–AUGUST 2021

New Daylight

Sustaining your daily journey with the Bible

Included in this issue
Secrets and mysteries in Mark ELIZABETH RUNDLE
Growing old DAVID RUNCORN
1 and 2 Timothy JANE WALTERS

Ideal for anyone wanting an accessible yet stimulating aid to spending time with God each day, deepening their faith and their knowledge of scripture. Each issue provides four months of daily Bible readings and comment, with a team of regular contributors drawn from a range of church backgrounds and covering a varied selection of Old and New Testament, biblical themes, characters and seasonal readings. Each daily section includes a short Bible passage (text included), thought-provoking comment and a prayer or point for reflection.

New Daylight
Sustaining your daily journey with the Bible
Edited by Sally Welch
£4.75 per issue
£18.00 one-year subscription (incl. postage)

brfonline.org.uk/new-daylight

Enabling all ages to grow in faith

Anna Chaplaincy

Living Faith

Messy Church

Parenting for Faith

The Bible Reading Fellowship (BRF) is a Christian charity that resources individuals and churches. Our vision is to enable people of all ages to grow in faith and understanding of the Bible and to see more people equipped to exercise their gifts in leadership and ministry.

To find out more about our ministries, visit

brf.org.uk